Amazing Olympic Athlete
WILMA RUDOLPH

AMAZING AMERICANS

Mary Dodson Wade

Enslow Elementary
an imprint of
Enslow Publishers, Inc.
40 Industrial Road
Box 398
Berkeley Heights, NJ 07922
USA

http://www.enslow.com

Enslow Elementary, an imprint of Enslow Publishers, Inc.
Enslow Elementary® is a registered trademark of Enslow Publishers, Inc.

Library of Congress Cataloging-in-Publication Data

Wade, Mary Dodson.
    Amazing Olympic athlete Wilma Rudolph / Mary Dodson Wade.
       p. cm. — (Amazing americans)
    Includes index.
    Summary: "This entry-level biography describes how Wilma Rudolph overcame childhood polio and competed in the Olympics"—Provided by publisher.
    ISBN-13: 978-0-7660-3282-8
    ISBN-10: 0-7660-3282-5
    1. Rudolph, Wilma, 1940—Juvenile literature. 2. Runners (Sports)—United States—Biography—Juvenile literature. 3. Women runners—United States—Biography—Juvenile literature. [1. African Americans—Biography—Juvenile literature.] I. Title.
    GV1061.15.R83W33 2009
    796.42092--dc22
    [B]   2008024890

Printed in the United States of America
072012 Lake Book Manufacturing, Inc., Melrose Park, IL

10 9 8 7 6 5 4 3

Caption: Wilma Rudolph at the Olympics in 1960.

CONTENTS

CHAPTER 1

Growing Up

Wilma Rudolph was born in a little town in Tennessee in 1940. Nobody thought the sickly baby would live. But Wilma grew up to become the fastest woman runner in the world.

◄ **Wilma Rudolph with the three gold medals she won at the 1960 Summer Olympics.**

Wilma's family was poor. When she was six, she had polio. The disease made her left leg and foot crooked.

Wilma's family helped her by rubbing her leg. They also took Wilma to the hospital to get her help.

All of her family's help paid off. At age nine, to everyone's surprise, she took off her brace and walked. By age 11, she was playing basketball at school. Her coach called her "Skeeter" because he said "you're little and fast and always in my way."

Wilma, on the right, standing with her older sister ▶
Yvonne. Wilma was six when this photo was taken.

CHAPTER 2

The 1956 Olympics

In high school, Wilma became a basketball star. She set the state record for the most points scored in a high school game.

Wilma ran faster than anyone else in high school, too. At age 16, she went to the Olympic games in Melbourne, Australia. She and her team won a bronze medal in the 4x100 meter relay.

◄ **Wilma Rudolph, second from left, holding her bronze medal with her teammates.**

The track coach at Tennessee State University gave her a scholarship to help pay for college. Wilma studied hard to become a teacher. Her coach made her work hard too.

Wilma, right, came in second to her teammate ▶
at this race.

CHAPTER 3

The 1960 Olympics

In 1960, Wilma went to the Olympics again. The day before her first race, she hurt her ankle. Wilma raced anyway. She ran faster than any woman ever had before.

Wilma set a record in her second race too.

◄ **Wilma Rudolph won the 100-meter race at the 1960 Olympics.**

In her third race, Wilma was the last runner on her relay team. She almost dropped the baton. Runners from other teams raced by. Wilma ran harder. The judges had to study a picture to see who won.

It was Wilma's team! They had set a world record. And Wilma had won three gold medals.

Wilma Rudolph crossed the line first. ▶
Her team won the relay race!

CHAPTER 4

Wilma the Teacher

Wilma finished college, then taught school. She later married and had four children. She helped coach young runners. But sadly, Wilma became sick with brain cancer.

◄ **Wilma Rudolph graduated from college in 1963. She wanted to be a teacher.**

Wilma Rudolph died when she was only 54 years old. Her flying feet were not always so fast. But her hard work and determination made her a champion.

Rudolph, right, hugs Florence Griffith Joyner, ▶ another runner. Joyner was a star of track and field. She won four Olympic medals.

SOMETHING TO THINK ABOUT

Wilma Rudolph was the first American woman to win three gold medals in the Olympics. She said, *"No matter what accomplishments you make [big things you do], somebody helps you."*

Wilma's college track coach was her friend for the rest of her life. Who else helped her?

Wilma Rudolph said, *"Triumph can't be had without the struggle."* She meant that you must work hard to win a race or do a good job.

What things happened in her life to show that is true?

TIMELINE

1940—June 23, born near Clarksville, Tennessee.

1946—Learned that she had polio.

1956—Won bronze medal at the Olympic Games in Australia.

1960—Won three gold medals at Olympic Games in Rome, Italy.

1963—Finished college and married Robert Eldridge. She taught elementary school and coached the high school track team.

1994—November 12, died in Nashville, Tennessee.

Words to Know

brace—A metal piece put on the leg (or other body part) to support bones or make them straight.

cancer—A disease.

Olympics—An athletic contest held every four years in a different country. Athletes from many nations compete in them.

relay race—A race in which each member of a team runs only a certain part of the distance.

scholarship—Money given to help a student continue his or her studies.

track—Running or jumping sports, also the place where runners race.

LEARN MORE

BOOKS

Braun, Eric. *Wilma Rudolph*. Mankato, MN: Capstone, 2005.

Krull, Kathleen. *Wilma Unlimited: How Wilma Rudolph Became the World's Fastest Woman*. San Diego: Harcourt Brace, 1996.

INTERNET ADDRESSES

Roberts, M.B. "Rudolph Ran and the World Went Wild"
http://espn.go.com/sportscentury/features/00016444.html

Wilma Rudolph: Overcoming Childhood Handicaps
http://www.olympic.org/wilma-rudolph

PLACES TO VISIT

National Women's Hall of Fame
76 Fall Street
P.O. Box 335
Seneca Falls, NY 13148
Phone (315) 568-8060

INDEX

A

Australia, 9

B

basketball, 6, 9

brain cancer, 17

O

Olympics, 9, 13–14

P

polio, 6

R

relay race, 9, 14

Rudolph, Wilma, 5–6, 9–10, 13–14, 17–18

T

Tennessee State University, 10